ADDITIONAL
FIGHT OR FLIGHT

"I read *Fight or Flight* in one wide-eyed-and-wondrously-rapt sitting, but that doesn't mean I won't return often to this miraculously uplifting book of lost and found romantic and familial love. McFadyen-Ketchum's soul-lifting poems are flooded with bird song, hoodoos, planets, leaping spiders, coyotes, and watchful crows, to name a few. What begins as a desperate, desolate solo camping trip ends with a new love's "hand / Pressed hard / To this pained man's heart." With their foxglove, star-nosed moles, and glowing snakes, these poems will fill you with renewed reverence for worldly and celestial splendors. McFadden-Ketchum takes us on an unforgettable journey from despair to joy, from utter aloneness to a life teeming with love and light."

—Martha Silano, *Gravity Assist*
and *The Little Office of the Immaculate Conception*

FIGHT OR FLIGHT

Andrew McFadyen-Ketchum

STEPHEN F. AUSTIN STATE UNIVERSITY PRESS

For more information:
Stephen F. Austin State University Press
P.O. Box 13007 SFA Station
Nacogdoches, Texas 75962
sfapress@sfasu.edu
www.sfasu.edu/sfapress

Managing Editor: Kimberly Verhines
Book Design: Emily Williams
Cover Art: Siolo Thompson
Cover Design: Emily Williams
Distributed by Texas A&M Consortium
www.tamupress.com

ISBN: 1-978-1-62288-943-3

ACKNOWLEDGMENTS

"The Dying Park": *Bat City Review*, Issue 19

"Catch & Release": *Non-Binary Review*, Winter 2022

"Raising The Dead": *Atticus Review*, Winter 2022

"Rejoice": *I-70 Review*, Fall 2023

"Heaven-Fire": *Vox Populi*, Fall 2022

"A Good Man": *Vox Populi*, Fall 2022

"The Toddler": *Vox Populi,* Fall 2022

"On Earth": *Bluestem*, May 2019

"Want": *Bending Genres,* Issue 15, June 2020

"Lure": *CULTURAL DAILY*, January 2021

"The Lie": *CULTURAL DAILY*, January 2021

"My Father's Sneeze": *CULTURAL DAILY*, January 2021

"Another World": *MiGoZine*, Spring 2020

"Whooping Crane": *MiGoZine*, Spring 2020

"A Trio of Crows": *MiGoZine*, Spring 2020,

"A Trio of Crows": nominated for a 2021 Pushcart Prize by *MiGoZine*

"Falling Into Fire" as "Moonset": *Iron Horse Literary Review*, 15.2
(Spring 2013): 22-23

"With You": *storySouth*, Issue 50, Fall 2020

"Home": *storySouth*, Issue 50, Fall 2020

CONTENTS

I. Forgiveness

II. The Unborn

III. Beautiful Dreams

For my Karen, Eli, Otis, and Siliuna

"Stay alive, no matter what occurs. I will find you.
No matter how long, no matter how far—I will find you."

–Hawkeye, *Last of the Mohicans*

I. Forgiveness

On Earth

If the dead don't know how on earth to live,
How on earth can the living? Mistakes stack up
Like nights. We get in over our heads whether
Or not we truly love the ones we're with.
No one asks to be dropped onto the glass like this
And though we do not rehearse our deliveries,
We find ourselves delivered nonetheless into these
Thin-skinned vessels we call the Self in which
We love and lose and love and lose again
And again, and must learn to trust the stars are fixed
In the ether despite our first fevers, our mothers
Either wringing their hands over us in our cribs
Through the night or trusting our illness burns
Brightly, yes, but nowhere near as brightly as us.

Want

A wind descended from the west
     To rattle the orchard trees. Placards

Shaped like dogtags or thumbs
     Lashed to apples and plums

Rang out as though wine flutes struck
     At the marriage table. Cluster after cluster of star-

Tiny white blossoms let go their limbs
     And laid themselves

Across the river—the gush of spring,
     The railing wind, the clanging of the trees

So loud, not a soul could make out
     The nuthatches and cardinals battling

The zephyrs and westerlies
     To take their place among the planets

To throat their earth-bound song.

A Trio of Crows

A trio of crows followed him all that afternoon
Through the canyonlands of Utah's Fiery
Furnace, a place people go to get lost

Because they believe they will be found.
From the salt-white peaks of the hoodoos,
The crows trumpeted and hawked. Backlit

By the sun, the crows sputtered and cawed.
Wings closed or splayed before the gray day moon,
They hoped, the man knew, he'd either drop food

Or become food, yet still, he felt…Protected?
Companioned? Watched over, somehow,
No matter the way? *Is this all I desire?*

He wondered as he squeezed through a slot
In stone: Anyone, any*thing*, to watch over me,
No matter their will, their intent, or skill?

Is that all I need, he asked the crows' shadows,
The high cliff faces, the sun going down
As he pondered turning back—*Any manner of flight*

No matter how wrecked or rapt its wings?

On the First Anniversary of Divorce

He wakes before light from difficult dreams.
He rises from bed and thus from sleep.
He drives to the Casey's for weak coffee
And cigarettes, then on to the lake
On the map to catch the cardinal's song.
There, the last of the fog is burning off.
A reed stretches so far from the bank
It nearly touches its reflection's face.
The heady scent of lilac enters and exits him.
His heart opens and closes again, and again.
Why must I wake? he asks his face on the water.
Why must I dream? he asks the face of his father.

He'd woken before light, after all, from his dreams.
He'd risen from bed and thus from sleep.
He'd driven to the Casey's for weak coffee
And cigarettes, then on to the lake
On the map to catch the cardinal's song.
There, he'd watched the last of the fog's burning off,
A reed had stretched so far from the bank
It nearly touched its reflection's face.
The heady scent of lilac had entered and exited him.
His heart had opened and closed again, and again.
Why must I wake? he'd asked his face on the water.
Why must I dream? he'd asked the face of his father.

He woke, didn't he, before light from a dream?
He rose from bed, did he not, and thus from sleep?
He drove to the Casey's for weak coffee

And cigarettes, then on to the lake
On the map to catch the cardinal's song.
There, the last of the fog was gone.
A reed stretched so far from the bank
It nearly touched its fate.
The heady scent of lilac became him.
His heart beat again, and again, and again.
Why must I wake? he asked his face on the water.
Why must I dream? he asked the face of his father.

8.9 Acres

The moment the papers are finally signed, he drives
Straight to Judy's 8.9 acres with a twelve-person
Walmart tent and nowhere else to go.
She helps him find some level ground

Beneath a black walnut. Together, they follow
The diagrams to raise the tent's walls.
They pay out fifty feet of orange electrical
Cord from her bedroom window so he can brew

Coffee in the morning, have a little light
At night. After an early supper of homegrown
Veggie stew, they walk the property, feed
The chickens, pick hornworms on all-fours

From the tomato plants and place them
Gingerly at the bases of sweetgums
Or in the tall wild grasses populated by bees.
She loans him her dog's double mattress wet

With flea spray and a high-powered flashlight
To ward off foxes and owls that stalk
The chicken coop each night then offers
A gun as a joke, "For protection!" she says,

"This is Trump country, you know."
The man says thank you but no
And enters the tent that first night.
Wrapped in his mother's quilt

On the mattress on the gray tarp floor,

He listens to the pang of treefrogs and locusts,
The barking of dogs chained to stumps,
The slow descent into evening and sleep.
Next morning, with the rising of first light
And the songs of the birds scientists theorize
Is code for "I survived the dark! I survived
The dark! Did you? Did you? Survive the dark?

The dark?!" it takes the man a moment
To piece together where he is: Judy's property
In Illinois. The tent. The woman
He married ten years ago never to roll over again

Onto her side and gaze into his eyes, the gun
That could be waiting for him beneath his pillow…
He does as the therapists instruct:
He names the cardinals, the wrens, the crows

And goldfinches by the calls they make.
He counts the leaping spiders scaling
The thin walls of his new home, composes
A list of all he is grateful for (the stars,

Strong coffee, dear friends), looks for shapes
In his breath climbing the air above him
And finds, as always, the children of his dreams—
The two little boys, the one little girl,

Dancing in the kitchen, swimming
In the ocean, crying in his arms
With first heartbreak—and he asks himself, "Why,
Oh why, did you not say 'Yes' to the gun?"

No Use

-After Sappho

It is no use, Mother Dear,
I cannot keep going.

Blame Sappho, if you must,
Fragmented as she was found.

Blame my marrying young.
Rain. The twenty-eight phases of the thirty-seven moons.

Blame the angels descending
With their swords on fire.

Mother, it is no use.
That girl who arrived

With a pool cue in her hand, naked
fingernails, a light in her eyes?—

That Syracuse girl in the baggy blue jeans
Carrying a degree in psychology?—

That girl who made me believe
She would make me a father?—

That girl has nearly killed me
With her love.

The Trouble with Light

Nights, when light retreats, the man's grief goes with it.

It is okay when it is dark to smoke a joint and lay around
Thinking about kinky sex while reading sci-fi paperbacks in bed.

Soon, he will be asleep and dreamless.

No visions of the wife he lost returning
To him through the tall grass. No more dreams
Of the children he believed her body
with its magic would bring him
Emerging from the sea.

Nights, he could be the only person on earth, let alone
In this twelve-person tent pitched on a friend's property
In Illinois, a twin mattress dank with the musk of wet dogs
To lay his head on. A broken lamp to read by.

Though a dog's barking, though the AMTRAK's AM coo
Through town, though the chickens' death-squawking in the dark
Often pulls him from sleep, grief rarely finds the man in the night.

This is the trouble with light—
The range of vision it brings:

The children he imagined. Their names.
The baggy sweatshirt and jeans she wore the night they met.

The last words she said to him: "I love you.
I will always love you."

Useless Human Things

The external hard drive housing
Twelve years of photographs
A decade of marriage
Finally dies
And there's nothing to do but dig it
A private grave
And drop it in without a sound

Nothing to do but take apart
That once-spinning disc of ones and zeroes
Screw by tiny screw
And wear each glowing diode
Each leaf-thin circuit
Around his neck like a prize

Nothing to do but drive out
To the Best Buy where for $69.95
They can tap into its mainframe
Transfer its data to the cloud
And swipe a card to fix a thing
That can never be unbroken

He'd like to place this metal
And plastic urn in the trash
With the coffee grounds
Soon to be trucked to the landfill
Where he can envision it
Far beneath the earth's surface
In a band of other 21st century relics

The remains of dinosaurs miles below
Further down
The first creatures
To emerge from the sea

This external hard drive
A black box of memory in the hands
Of the alien excavator who
Having dug it up alongside a flip phone
A coffee mug
A pair of perfectly good boots
Turns it over a moment
Inspects its ports clogged with mud
And taps on its shell
To see what lives inside

Then tosses it aside
With a huff
In a pile
Of all the other
Useless human things

Another World

I'd have done better had I been born
In the trees. If only I could breathe water,

Was at home wriggling my thin body
Through the earth, surfacing only

When it floods to nourish the hungry
Hatchling, lure for the rainbow trout.

If only I'd never met that girl
Born in the month of Saturn,

That ringed giant that nearly became
A star. Does Saturn dream too

Of another world in which it *is*
A star, mother-father to a solar system,

Its moons planets inhabited by creatures
Of its divine light? Do the wild things

I so yearn to be also grieve?
Does the creek bed weep

When rain returns?
Will I ever love,

Or be loved, like that
Again?

Sirius in February

That first night on the road to nowhere,
The man woke three times in the night,
Warm in his mummy bag and UGGs
Next to the fire ice cold in its ring.
Frost cracked as he rolled onto his back
To peer at what woke him: A wobbling
Blue light high in the southern sky—
Too massive for heavenly body,
Too still for space station or plane,
So bright it washed out the moon
Otherwise white-hot on the horizon.
The man didn't move a muscle
As he gazed at the night. The man
Didn't wiggle out of his bag
Into the colder-than-forecasted cold
He could read his breath by.
He did not retrieve the field glasses
From the car his father gifted him
Before his journey for "peering
At the stars." The man, instead,
Did nothing. He took it all in
The way he'd always wanted
But rarely could. The man breathed
And breathed and breathed
Then rolled back onto his side
To re-enter his night of difficult dreams.

Faith

It took longer than expected, the rise of the sun,
But it was brilliant, the silent traffic of contrails
That crisscrossed the sky, one of them heading

Due west as he gazed due east so that it appeared
To ascend the heavens like a spider burning on its thread,
Its fumes growing hotter and wider the higher

It climbed. Then the sun did rise or, more accurately,
The earth rolled over in its bed of stars so that our star
Appeared, at first, as a single point of light opening

Its eye upon the salt-rim of the horizon to fill it
With light. Detail upon detail emerged. The canyon below
Was suddenly articulate and vast and all species

Of color. The purple sage at his feet cast a shadow
And thus took on dimension. The sand at his feet
Was clearly constructed of particles the naked eye

Could now discern. A coyote yowled at his back
As the day's first stellar jays whined all around him.
"You can go on," the man said to himself as if

In the midst of a dialogue with it all. *The sun,*
He thought as the shadow of a raven passed over,
"Rises in the east. And the moon," he said aloud

As the raven itself alighted in a box elder,

"Leaves you somewhere in the west." When the raven
Ruffled its wings, its shadow ruffled its wings.

When the raven shifted its weight, the box elder
Rattled *like rain sticks*, he thought, "Like prayer,"
He said as he turned back to camp, "Like the faith,"

He uttered to the shadow of himself climbing the trail
Ahead of him, *That we will learn to love again.*

The Sea Lions

She loved all manner of wild animal:
In Mexico, no one could stop her
From feeding the rat-like Tejons
At the ruins. In Nevada, she nearly lost
A finger petting the wild stallions
Who grazed just inches from Rte. 208.
In Ireland, she simply would not stick
To high ground above the tidepools
Where the sea lions grazed in the sun,
"Like tube socks of flesh," the man joked
As they, three years married, picked
Their way away from the other tourists
On the shore. "Like sea slugs that have doffed
Their shells," he laughed as they skipped rock
To rock across the low tide until they stood
Within inches of those strange mammals
In the loosening light. Their dark skins
Kaleidoscoped with the weakening
Sun any time they moved. Their eyes
Blinked lazily as unhungry flytraps.
The wife made a joke of reaching out
To touch one, and the husband fell for it,
Snatching her hand from the air so quickly,
They nearly lost their balance and fell into
Each other, laughing. The tide,
They saw then, was coming in, opaque
And briny as it frothed around their boots,
Silently filling the dry gaps that made
Their way home. The man led the way back,

The woman he called "Little One"
That decade before he finally gave up
Too short to return on her own without sopping
Her feet. "I got you," he said as he spanned
The gaps too wide for her legs with his
And held her by the hips to lift her
Beyond the possibility of her own leaping
From dry spot to dry spot, the two of them
Like dancers on a stage so entranced by their routine,
By their work and rhythm, they were surprised
When they struck solid ground, not a stitch
Of them wet, the husband's hands firm
On the wife's waist, ready to aid her aloft
Or to fix her, whichever she chose,
Firmly to ground.

Forgiveness

When finally he tells his wife, his One
And Only, his Little One, that he can take

No more, she sinks into his lap, she leans
Into his ear, she kisses his neck, she weeps

And weeps and weeps and weeps
And says, "I know, my love, I know."

II. The Unborn

Broken White-Boy Heart

Who knows how to write about love or its loss—
And who cares? declares the voice in his head.
Write about important things, any*thing,* Sweet
Jesus, *but yourself.* Don't write about waking
Each morning from a dream with a gun,
Don't write about how that gun might taste
Pressed to the tongue: A nine-volt battery,
A rusted penny plucked from a wishing well
And placed like communion where it is to dissolve.
This man was married a decade *exactly,*
Some sort of sick cosmic joke to have to leave
Your wife on your ten-year anniversary—*But who,*
The voice reminds him, *gives a* good *goddamn?*
Today is six-hundred-ninety-seven days
Since the day he left, and counting. Gone
The pet rabbits. Gone the white dishes. Gone
The immersion blender wedding gift. Gone
The sweaters she bought him each Christmas
When he finally said "I must go"—*And what of it?*
The voice interjects. *So you're sad. So you're* [air
quotes] *"Traumatized." So you wake each morning
Reaching for her in the dark. So you want to die
Die die? So what you will never have a child?
So what you are not deserving of love? You know what
Your mother would say: There are starving children
In Africa. You know what Facebook would say:
Another cop killed another unarmed black man
Somewhere in silent America. Trust me,* the voice
That inhabits him says, *Stay silent. No one cares
About your broken, white-boy heart.*

Makeup

All the patrons at this Starbucks look so happy
Even he, the psychologist's son, is fooled.
A father stands before the front window brushing
His daughter's hair. A woman in thick-rimmed

Glasses, a paisley tie knotted high on her throat,
Smiles into a Dell. A college kid biking
Through the Denver gray releases great huffs
Of breath like joy. The man could have been,

Has been, could be all of them: The cyclist
Unaffected by cold, they who slips on wingtips
And knots a tie for work—how many times
Has he dreamed of brushing a daughter's hair?

In the bathroom mirror designed specifically
For his use, the man tries to unwrite the face
He finds there: Difficulty breathing from his cheeks,
Panic in crowds from crow's feet, the shadow

Of his loveless marriage from beneath his eyes.
He's always felt more She than He but has never
Written a stitch about it. Back in his seat,
He can't help but notice the play of light

On the woman's glasses, the daughter's gaze
Out the window, the cyclist long gone. It
Is April. It is snowing. Snow puddles the sidewalk.
Snow strikes the ground without a sound.

Fight or Flight

He's never understood them, they
Who wish to live forever: Vampire

Heartthrobs supping on blood over death,
Nazis obsessed with drinking from Jesus' cup,

All those Southern Sundays wasted on the divine.
He himself prefers endings: Line breaks

A way of conclusion, periods most holy
Punctuation. He likes to think he'd choose

Most any darkness over eternal light,
But if death is the cooling dark he imagines it

To be, why did his heart quicken,
His hands shake with sweat on that cliff face

In Virginia some twenty years ago
When his body swung away from the rock

Like a barn door on its hinge three hundred
Feet above earth, the end he believes he desires

Placed at his feet—an offer inked on a slip
of paper slipped beneath the door: Fight

Or flight on that precipice, and his fool heart
Chose to live. *Why didn't you let go*

When you had the chance? he asks himself
A lifetime later. *Why didn't you accept*

Such a plausible end?

First Swim

In the one story my mother tells,
I see my mother realize she's heard
Nothing from me, her toddler, for too long
When she rises from her lawn chair
By the city pool in the sun
To see her little boy in the clear
Chlorine blue, one of my arms raised
As if waving. In the one story
My mother tells about me,
She dives into the water full-clothed
In overalls to pull me from the warm deep
I slipped somehow, blessedly, heavenly
Gratefully into. She cradles me
In her arms as she rises from the water
Dripping from her like robes, my mother
A dark-haired Venus placing her son
On his favorite blanket next to the green
Plastic Stegosauruses and palms
As she coos at me and weeps and weeps.
O, how I wish she'd loved me so well
In the forty years hence
Or had taken a touch longer to realize
She'd lost sense of me, her boy.
Now, when she rises from her seat
On brilliant afternoons, awkward among
The other more-natural mothers
To see me in the deep end
Waving, waving—she simply stands
There and waves back and waves back,
Singing softly, singing lovingly
"Goodbye, my boy, goodbye."

Names In Winter

There was a time when the trees were not so silent.
Wind brought word from the faces of the cliffs.
Songbirds were certain of the meter of their verses.

Now, after so much, the dormant-gray grasses bend
In no direction particular. Night's braille speaks to no one.
And the trees? The trees have shed their one-thousand names.

The Orb Weaver's Song

Our orb weaver has passed on.
Come spring, countless of her children

Will hatch from the egg she's left behind—
A planet hovering in its cradle of silk,

A womb suspended in the porchlight's gleam.
Does she sing, I wonder, to her little ones

In her sleep? Do they sing back,
The unborn, in the midst of their dream?

Relief

When finally he tells the boy
He's imagined since childhood,
"We will never play catch in the yard,"
"I will never teach you how to change
Your oil or apologize to a woman,"
"I have failed to find a vessel for you,
My Little-Star, my Little Love,"
The boy forms his tiny hands into tiny fists
And rattles the air, he plays with his red
Truck in the corner by himself, A-Boy-
Already-Born pushes him from the swings,
A-Girl-Expected trips him in the dirt
Where he kicks and screams and spits for life
As the actual fathers at the playground
Shake their heads even though they know
There's nothing the man can do until
His Beautiful Boy, until his Little Mister,
Until his Mini-Me stumbles back to him
Exhausted as a drunk from his tantrum
And curls up in his arms, and looks up
At him and confesses, with his eyes,
His relief.

A Good Man

"Don't. Move. A muscle," my father says
To my sister, then rises from his place
At the table, strides down the hall to his office,
And opens and closes the door with a click.
I, my mother, and sister stare at the dinner table.
We examine the woodgrain, seek visions
From the swirling designs. If we're quiet
Enough, we pray, he'll fall back to his work.
If we don't make a sound, he will, we hope, forget.
Then we hear again the click open and shut
Of the door, his footsteps down the hall,
And he reappears in the kitchen with a pair
Of silver shears, the bronze screw of its hinge
The scared eye of an animal as he sits before
My sister, opens the scissors before her face,
And removes her bangs in a single snip.

My father is a good man. "Dad," I've said
To him some nights, "you were a good dad."
Yet, when I recall my sister's bangs falling
To the table so my father can see the truth or lie
In her eyes, I return to the scene he painted
The night I was 10 when he'd caught me stealing
"Yet again" and "for the last *goddamn* time":
My arrest, the prison they'd put me in,
The metal table they'd strap me to, the scissors
They'd use to un-man me "*just* like these,"
He said, holding those shears to the light.

To this day, my sister and I wonder if Dad
Got it right. "Fear," he explained years later,
"Is sometimes the only tool." "And I did, after all,"
My sister says, "confess. And my bangs?
They grew back." "And I did," I admit, "apologize
To everyone I stole from…and look how proud
Dad is of me now." But then there are
My sister's eyes after Dad's removed her hair,
Green and still as the eyes of a predator.
Then there's Mom, my sister reminds me,
"our *mother*," sitting quietly in her seat,
Her hands folded silently in her lap.

The Dying Park

It was Chris who first saw
The glowing snake
That lazed across the alley
Between the Save-a-Lot
Parking lot and the park
Where our pets went to die:
A kingsnake, Chris believed
At least six feet in its dozing
Length, its chain-link
Of black scales
Magically aglow.

They approached the thing
At first with stealth,
Seven skinny kids
In their swimsuits
And scabs, picking at it
At first with sticks
Then with the tips
Of their Payless
Jordans and Deions
Until, emboldended
By stillness, they double-
Dog dared each other
Into leaping its stalled
Machinery—boys proving
They were men to girls proving
They weren't afraid
Uh nothin.

Day turned to night
In that alley. The sun
Shut down and the moon
Rose up, the children's faces
So brightly lit by snakeglow
They looked like cities
In the dark. And though
He should have seen
It coming, the boy flinched
When Sam's foot
Slammed down
On the snake's sparkling head
And Tim grabbed hold
Its writhing tail
And Chris slit it open
From anus to head
To see what that king
Was made of.

What did they find within?
A family of seven gray mice
Agleam with an even
More powerful light.
One mouse per child,
They fished each glowing
Body from snakemeat
And held them like jewels
In their hands. *Which*
Glowed first, the boy
Wondered, *Snake…*
Or the mice it ate?
And who would believe them

Or in all of that glow—
Like stars, Emma said,
Like JeeeeeeeSus, Sam said,
Like something
From another world,
Chris added as he began
To bring his bright blade
Down again *to see*
What glowed deeper in.

That's when, all at once
Their mouse eyes opened
And with a blaze
Of light and a newborn's
Wail, the mice leapt
From their hands to scatter
Into the green world
Of the dying park.
For some time,
Those kids just stood there,
Chris with knife poised
Above his irradiating
Palm, Sam's mouth
Agape, a streak
Of what looked like the guts
Of a firefly smeared
Across Cassie's shirt,
The snake hanging
From Tim's grip
In black ribbons and blood.

What had they witnessed,
They wondered as they washed
What glow remained
From their hands
In the creek that flowed
Between stormdrains
Beneath I-40, that bright
Substance briefly illuminating
The dark water with a seam
Of light that snaked
Into the mouth
Of the sewer system.

Were those mice
Resurrected? the boy wondered
The rest of the way
Home and the rest
Of his life…Or had they
Merely caught them dreaming
When they unzipped that king's
Belly and gathered them
In their hands?

The boy has dreamt
Many times of those
Glowing mice.
He often wakes
To floating down a river
In the dark
Submerged in the glow,
Fish darting like shooting stars
All around him,

The body of that snake
Bobbing on the water
Before him, which he gathers
In his hands and paddles
Back to the bank
And lays it on its back
And pulls the sides
Of its split belly together
Like stitching a wound,
Like swaddling a newborn,
Like jacketing a toddler
Eager to play in the snow.
Then he coos at the snake
Limp in his arms.
Then he gets back in the water.
The glow is gone
But cannot be far.
If he swims hard enough
With his one free arm,
Perhaps he can find it again.
Keep moving, he tells himself
As the undertow builds.
Keep moving, he tells himself
As he feels the child unraveling
In his arms. *Keep moving,*
He tells himself over and over.
What else is there to do?

Confession

When at last the man explains
To the toddler he has yearned for all his life
That "You, my Son, will never become
A threenager," "I will never take you,
To the park despite the rain," "I will never
Introduce you to a new bedtime story
For I, my Baby-Moon, for I,
My Sweet-Tot have failed to find
A mother with whom to make you,"
The boy balls his toddler hands
Into toddler fists and pounds them
Against the ground until they turn purple
As beets, he opens his mouth and wails
Like a siren, he pushes A-Girl
In-Diapers from the swings,
He kicks A-Boy-Just-Baptized
In the dirt, he tantrums and tantrums
Beneath the monkey bars for life
As all the fathers at the playground
Shake their heads, but there's nothing
The man can do until his Beautiful-
Imagined-Boy, His Son-As-Attainable-
As-Speaking-To-A-Star stumbles back
Into his lap, cheeks snotty with tears,
And curls up in his arms—quiet
As a seashell, quiet as a grieving—
And confesses, with his eyes, his relief.

Luck

Night balks. The cirrus shrug their shoulders.
The moon tears bright, white sheets of tissue paper
From the clouds and lays them out like tarot:
The Magician, The Fool, The Reaper's curved sickle.

Later, they'll call it a moonset—2 AM, stumbling
Home, the pale globe of a woman's knee
Slipping through skirts of cloud. Seems strange
To him now how long it took to derive a word
For that image, "Like a sunset," he said,
"But...*the moon*" up there, imbibing the sky.

Then, he didn't know how lucky he was to be alive
Only hours after bearing witness to the first forest fire
To sweep through Linville Gorge in a decade.

Barely twenty years old, he'd clung to the cliff face,
Anchored a mere hundred feet above the flames
That slithered through narrow leaf and pond pine
As he sucked in the few pockets of air he could find,
His partner tethered out of sight above him,

Terrified the fire's heat would snap the ropes
From which they hung, that their gear so carefully placed
In fissures and cracks would pop loose like teeth
From a burning body until the heat receded and its smoke lifted
To reveal the trees below, naked and sinewy
As bent ends of wire, the sky dark as tar paper.

Whatever faith he had then in stone and steel is gone,
But an image remains of the peregrine falcons he watched
Drop ahead of the fireline to feed on the field mice
And voles who fled the earth, baked and aflame.

How could anyone blame them for celebrating their lives
After that? Amber shots of liquor lined up on the bar.
Already exaggerating the details of their story as they smoothed
Dollar bills on the hard edge of the jukebox and sang along

To the clichés of Tom Petty as though they had voices—
"And I'm freeeeeee, free faaaalllinnnn!"—car keys fished
From his pocket by the pretty bartender who refused
His certainly obnoxious pleas for her name before finally
They made their way home beneath that "moonset" sky.

Now, when the moon rises to skip its pinpoints of light
Off the spangled shingles of rooftops, now, when the moon
Illuminates the otherwise dark heights of maples
And calls forth his dream of fire, he's not so lucky.

The ropes weaken with heat. A crucial anchor pops.
Something above snaps. His lungs fill with smoke,
And he can hold on no longer... But when he falls,

It's not towards the lit wicks of treetops, the hot kiln
Of the earth not rushing toward him but, instead, away—
One of those swift raptors having gathered him mid-fall
As prey and now the hillsides and pastures dropping away,

The sky darkening with night, the crisscrossing deltas
And rivers and whitecaps to the west he so loves

Turning the color of blood as last light funnels
Between the peaks like a spirit taking leave of its body,
And he, this boy, this man-to-be, can finally breathe.

The Lie

Their father has been silent
For minutes at his spot
At the dinner table,
His sister logicking
Her way through
Another lie,
Their mother washing
The dishes,
When something
She says shifts
The animal
Behind his eyes,
And he brings
His fist down so hard
On the table,
It sends the silver
Mixing bowl
Of raspberry jam
Flying into the air,
The kitchen's bright
Yellow walls
"Dripping,
With what looked,"
His sister says
Years later,
"Like blood."

Raising The Dead

The first time he buries his dead pet bird,
The boy digs him up two nights later.

Think March in Tennessee. The calls
Of spring peepers. An AM rain.

Like a God, like a father, like a lover,
The boy had lorded over Bud, short for bud-

Gerigar, that house bird known for human speech
He and his father purchased

From the pet store between the Sir Pizza
And Goodwill just days before

To ward off his loneliness. The boy began
With the *Webster's Pocket*, clearly enunciating

The day's vocabulary, the particulars
Of each word's pronunciation.

When that failed to rouse Bud to speech,
He read etymologies aloud from the skin-thin *OED*.

When still the bird did not speak,
The boy played audiobooks he borrowed

From the public library while he slept: *A Tale
Of Two Cities*. Stephen King's *IT*. *All's Well*

That Ends Well. Every night for a week
He read passages from the "Good Book"

His grandmother gifted him for turning
Twelve he otherwise only opened

For its illustrations of apostles and slaves,
The horned beasts and serpents

Entering the ark in mating pairs.
Finally, the boy told Bud stories he conjured

All his own, but if Bud ever spoke
It was in his own tongue—so loud

And clear and trilling through one
Particularly dark night, it woke

The boy from his dream, and, as if
He were still in the dream, he reached

Into the cage and closed his hands
Around Bud's wings to recite the Ten

Commandments, and when he reopened
His hands, found Bud unmoving.

Twenty-five years later, ten years
of failed marriage later, the boy now a man

Nearly unhinged at thirty-seven
Will be awoken within a nightmare

Of playing with the children he never made,
Of begging that girl he loved and married

To come home, *please just come home.*
He will tiptoe as the boy he once was

Through the eyes of the man he has become
In the way things can only be in dreams

Past his parent's bedroom, down the hall,
And out the front door to his mother's garden

Where he and his father laid Bud to rest.
The man-child will kneel before the white cross

Of two orangesicle sticks and a twist tie.
He will reach into the rain-wet soil to lift

From the earth the Dollar General
Tupperware in which he placed Bud's

Boy-broken body. He will crack open the lid
Of Bud's plastic coffin and will begin with

Strange motions of his hands like wings.
Then he'll click his tongue, will whistle through

Clenched teeth. Does he believe he can match
The whines and coos of a bird

No longer breathing? Does this man
Believe that if he calls his ex-wife,

She will answer? How to make
A dead dream flare back to life?

Why else come here in person or nightmare?
Why else cup the ones we have loved

And lost so sweetly in our hands?

Mercy

When finally he tells the infant girl
He's met so often in his dreams,

"I will never watch you take
Your first steps, My Noodle-Neck,"

"I will never learn to change your diaper,
My Stinker-Doo," "I will not watch you

Learn to smile while hovering
Over you in bed in that cabin in Indiana

With your mother, your beautiful mother,
My Little-Loony-Toony, for

I can take no more," the man's Bunny-Bop,
His Honey-Bunny crawls to him

In her onesie with the snaps,
She climbs into his lap,

And he reads to her her favorite book,
And he sings to her her favorite song,

And she buries her head in his chest,
And her heart flutters in its brilliant cocoon,

As she coos and coos
Herself to sleep.

My Father's Sneeze

So loud
And violent
And emulative
Of his rage
One once
Startled
The man
The boy
The child
So much
He snapped
The Number 2
Pencil
In his hand
In half
Its sharp point
Of graphite
Piercing
The flesh
Of his palm—
A mark
Left inside
No scarring
Could cure.

Happiness

"I never was one of them,"
He wants to write of the happy
Line of children leaping puddle
To puddle on their way to school,
All neon laces and superhero
Backpacks, the rain descending
So delicately through the trees,
It's almost imperceptible to the eye—
Their joy, he thinks, *a sort of instinct.*

But how, he checks himself there
On his best friend's porch
In Denver a week into divorce
As the children shuffle and dance
Dizzily as happy drunks
Through the rain so soft
It is better perceived by ear than sight, *How*
Can I claim anything anymore
And know it to be true?

Which takes him, somehow,
To the creatures that buzzed
And thrummed in the trees
Of his backyard when he
Was still a boy, and he entered
The dark to climb his way
To them, hand over hand,
Limb by limb up the night tree
Where, instead of entering

The singing he sought, he entered
The silence his entering made
And was forced to wait
So long for their singing
To return that he fell asleep
Straddling an oak limb
And woke to falling, crying out
As if from a nightmare
For any arms to catch him—

Again: the instinct he used to trust,
Yet here he is failing
To follow it under a rain so slight
It barely upsets the aspens
As "I never was" becomes
I don't know, and "one
Of them" becomes *like them*,
"if I ever was" falling silently,
Infinitely, instinctively, in-between.

III. Beautiful Dreams

Home

He wakes to the tapping
Of his Lover's finger
On his chest:

A bluebird opening
A shell, a watchmaker
Tinkering a gear.

"You were talking again
In your sleep," she says,
Her face inches above his.

"You kept saying
'I can't wait to go home;
I can't wait to go home.'

'Don't you get it, My Love,'
I wanted to say, 'We *are*
Your home. We are.'"

All The Things I Do Not Know

In one square foot of winter leaves
Collected in the river, in an eye blink
Of shallow curling ebb—all the things
I do not know. The must and musk
Of thyme. Red's deep raspberry. Cold's
Deep brick. Those meant to reproduce
And their carriers. Seed pods seeking
A bank, warm soil their final resting place
And home. A rich perfume rises
From leaves long and thin—fingers
Born for the piano's keys. Orange rays
Shine through a blue-wet sky, yellow
Simmering to umber with December's
Scalding cold, tiny floating metropolis
In this single square foot of Caney Fork
Tributary rarely worth mention
On the state or county maps we unfold
Across the dash, driving with one knee,
Coffee searing our hands, searching
For the next unfished hole, a galaxy
Clockwise turning in the middle
Of the world on the edge of the Milky
Way, backwash habitat powered
By the river's flow north to south—
In this one elbow of creek, in this
Flashbulb instance of life,
Of this happy, O harried life—
All thing things I do not know.

With You

All night, they mistook
The white bat who dropped
In and out of the darkness
And light of a lamp post
For a meteor shower
Pouring from the stars
That would not give up.
It wasn't the first time
They'd mistaken one thing
For another: Good lovers
For wine, a beautiful lie
For truth, yet another house finch
For some form more rare
From the pages of the guidebook.
But why be disappointed? they asked
One another in the night,
For they were together sipping
Rosé below Jupiter in a hot tub
In the middle of the woods
In the middle of COVID
In the middle of their lives
On the eve of her thirty-ninth
Circuit around the sun. In hours,
They plan to wake in the cabin
They've rented to make love.
Then they will rise naked
From the warm sheets to seek
Neptune through the telescope,
That god of freshwater

Who will be outshone by Mars
And the quarter moon. "Isn't that
How life is?" he'll remark
As she strains her eye
Against the lens, adjusting
And readjusting the focus ring
to no avail—her strawberry blonde
mess of curls falling around
Her shoulders, her breasts
In moonlight—"Life,
This constant search for water.
Each day a journey"—he'll take
Her hand, he'll kiss down
Her body and will say
Eyes open, looking up
Into hers, "Each day a journey
That ends and begins,
Thank God, with you."

Night Terrors

I know my Lover has awoken
From nightmare when she leaps
From bed and runs for the door
As if she is escaping her father.
I've learned to wait for her return,
Out of breath and chill with sweat,
Having placed her hands
On the children's chests to check
Their breathing in their cribs
Before slipping back beneath
The covers with me—her breasts,
Her back, her hair, her heart,
That man, that evil man—where she
Places her head on my heart
And breathes in and out, and in
And out, until she falls again
To what, I pray, are beautiful dreams.

Something More Suitable

Please My Love dig a hole
In the earth

And drop me inside
And bury me over with earth

And build a fire where I lie
And wait for my return

As a red-winged blackbird
As white noise

As a drop of water
On the tip of a leaf

And I will come to you
Each night

And I will sing to you
Each night

And no one but you will know
I am still here

Upon Death

I would like to have been a bird,
A small black one with white
Speckles along the spines of my feathers,
Those always seen in large number
Picking seed on the hillsides
From between the billion blades
Of grass. I would like, Lord,
To have been a member of my flock
Who could fly from pine to elm
To oak to wire from temple
To steeple to bridge, no yes
No maybe no yet, only this rise
And fall from earth to sky
And back again as if led
By one mind, a single spirit
Eternal, a life shared
By my multitude—Mother,
Father, Sister, Wife, Neighbor,
Husband, Boss, Cousin, God, My God,
Make me one before I try to fly.

Whooping Crane

The man doesn't know why he's come to the lake.
Six days straight he's woken from hard dreams—
"Melodramatic," he says to himself, "nothing
Anyone wants to read about," thus his drive
To the ice to pick his way through the trees.

He doesn't know it yet, but he's come for me,
The white whooping crane he spots looking back
Over a shoulder as I rise from the margin
Of the lake with one, two flaps of my wings.

He stops, transfixed midstep, my movement
Through sunlight transforming my flight
Into blades of blinding light, my swim
Through the sky becoming a disappearing
As I blend, like time, into the sycamores.

This is when he sees them: The deer tracks
Cast in the ice-hard mud, the day moon
Inhabiting the clouds. This is when he hears
Them: The chit-chit of chickadees, the squawking

Gang of jays. Now the man can smell
Fresh earth on the wind, now the man
Can smell the coming snow, now he can accept
His Lover's love—the world he inhabits
Made so loud by my rise, it shines.

The Call of the Pileated Woodpecker

Like laughter, true,
But don't tell him it's not yearning
My ratcheting through the trees.

Laughter in particular
Turns desperate when you lock a winged thing
Like me in a cage:

Longing. Love. Desire.
His hands cupping her face
For a kiss.

Her hand
Pressed hard
To this pained man's heart.

Rejoice

You see what you think
Is a red-tailed hawk
On the wing then hear
Its caw and realize
It is only a crow.
Why only? My children
Will reach for any source
Of light: Sirius beaming
In the South, a jet plane
Bearing passengers tearing
Through the night.
Worry not, I've learned.
Wait long enough
And a raptor will appear
In the bone-blue sycamores
Of any season. Given
Enough time and the danger
You desire will present
Itself. Rejoice, for now,
The crow. Rejoice the safety
Of a murder's shadow.
Rejoice the common.
Rejoice the cold.

Every Living Thing

A bird calls, and the mind assigns it
A name, draws the passerine's red crest,
Its beak designed for seeds,
How it bends the limb in which it sings.

He hears the bird but makes no move
To confirm what the ear believes.

Instead, he stays seated, fixed
To the ground his people do not come from
Amidst the pang of roofing hammers,
The barking of squirrels, the whine
Of insects and power lines—

Every straight line in sight
Hewn by human hands,
The word in every living thing.

Lure

She flicks her foot
In a ray of light
The way my father
Taught me to draw
A trout with a flick
Of my lure
From the shadows
And shallows.
She draws me
To her surface.
She pulls me
From the waters
I cannot breathe.
She kisses me tenderly
As I thumb open
My father's knife,
Its steel flashing
In the light the way
Steel flashes
In the light. "This
Is how you clean
A fish," I tell her son
As he adds his tears
To the river, this
First catch of his life
Becoming in my hands
His first kill. "This
Is my heart," I say
To his mother.

"Take it. Do with it
What you will.
You are the last woman
I will love."

The Hammer's Strike

Do the wild things find each other beautiful?
Does the buck gaze upon the doe, pluck
Forget-me-nots, hoove messages of love
In the streambed for her to find?
Does the heart of the rainbow trout
Quicken with the sight of the season's first
Turning leaves? Do mother robins push
Their fledglings from the nest and think,
"Beautiful! Just…beautiful!" I hope not.
For this means a world in which the star-
Nosed mole knows, one day, her children
Will die. This means a world in which
The black leach murders the hornworm
To take his wife, in which the red fox yearns
For deeper caves, the foxglove for more
Effulgent bells, that church bells pray for song
Without the pang of the hammer's strike.
"Leave that to us," I say to the tittering
Tit mice and doves. "Leave that to me,"
I will say to my Lover's eldest son
Struggling with rage in our arms.
"Let's make a new world together,"
I will say to his mother when he quiets
Into sleep. "Can't we stay the hand
Of the fisherman woken early
For the stream? Surely we can teach
Our boy how never to cry, how never
To feel pain. Tell me, Sweet Thing,
We can catch each fledgling
Before it fails to open its wings."

Heaven-Fire

Our middle child sings "Jingle Bells! Jingle Bells!"
Well into February when he wakes in his crib
Before his mother and I, his stepfather, have come
To change his diaper and help him into clothes,
And all he has to do is sing. The boy is not my blood
Though "Son" is the only name I have for "He-
Who-Will-Dance-To-Just-About-Anything," "Son-
Whose-Heart-His-Mother-Believed-Was-Broken-
Until-The-Doctors-Inspected-Its-Chambers-
And-Valves-To-Declare-Him-Fit," "Sweet
Ndee Boy," "Sweet Inupiaq Boy," "Sweet-Caroler-
In-The-Morning's-Half-light," "My heart beats
Just like yours," I want to write to him in the half-light
Of the kitchen, "your song seemingly serenading
The sun through the thin walls of this home we share
On 2nd Street, the same sort of blood circulating
Through our systems as daylight filters
Through the invasive hackberries in which the Emperors
Rest their wings, the same sort of blood, Son,
Feeding the same sorts of muscles as a whisper
Of a door opening down the hall halts your singing,
Stills your stepfather (who is only doing his best)
In the middle of his next line, the same saline
Solution of tears—no matter the record of massacres
And broken treaties between our peoples' histories
Brought to our sometimes-green/sometimes-blue
Eyes when the mother we both love in our different ways
Appears in the doorway, just-risen and without-
Coffee, her hair flaming down from the root like heaven…
Like fire…Like heaven-fire. Like life! Like life!"

The Toddler

Almost anything will break
The toddler's heart: His mommy's keys
Singing from the bowl of loose ends
And change on her way out the door
For work. Going to bed. Taking a bath.
Getting the *exact* snack he just asked for…
When the man rubs the boy's golden head
And says goodbye before he leaves him
At daycare, the child weeps, and the man
Must pick him up next to his wooden cubby,
And he must hold the toddler boy beneath
The colorful watercolors, and he must pat
His back with his hand, he must kiss
His golden Ndee head with his lips
And must say, in this order: "Don't worry,
Little One. Don't worry. I'll be back.
Daddies always come *right back.*"

On A Tuesday Near Midnight

"You wake, you take,"
The man's Lover says,
Before he enters the room
Where they love one another
And watch Netflix in bed,
And there she is, Little Siliuna,
Their daughter who is not his
But is, asleep in the crib
The man assembled the night
Before with a butter knife.
Her name is her father's
Peoples' word for the sky,
The weather, all those stories
Diagrammed by the stars.
She has dark hair. Her eyes
Are so black, they shine,
Her skin a brown that makes the man
Pound his chest when he thinks
Of what the world might do to her.
But not tonight. Tonight,
Over the gurgle of the noise
Machine's mechanical stream,
He hears her sing what sounds
Like a lullaby as she sleeps.
Cooing, she dreams.
"You only write about trouble,"
Her mother, the man's Lover,
Has joked, so he sits on the floor
Beside her daughter, *Your daughter,*

She insists, tired out
On a Tuesday near midnight
On another troubling day in America,
And he writes about this lovely
Little girl who is not his
But is and who he loves
As he prays and prays and prays
She too loves him.

Catch & Release

When finally it was time for our child
To arrive, I was not allowed to enter
The hospital room reserved for those
With your last name. Instead,
I went fishing, stayed by the phone
All that afternoon as I hunted for those
Who breathe water—biding my time
Until your text that would tell me
The little girl I'd call daughter
Had been born. My friends on the Buffalo
Tried to hide their perplexion.
They could not understand why a man
Without children could fall so in love
With a woman expecting a child "not his."
Is any child really "ours?"
And how rare is it really for a man
To dream of cradling the woman
He loves as she nurses the child
Who has only just become?
I caught a 23-inch smallmouth that day,
Biggest catch of my life. Five minutes
Of struggle just to catch a glimpse
Of that goliath of the shadows.
Another ten before I held it aloft
By the gills for a picture then prepared it
For release. The metaphor's lost
On neither of us: That little girl born
That morning the exact same size
As that smallmouth I gave back
To the water at day's end. Truth is,

I ate that fish, brought home four fat filets
I cooked four different ways for that
Ndee mama—pan-fried, deep-fried, broiled,
And grilled—the meat my Lover's body took in
Fed back to her child, "our child,"
She said as she lay on the bed
That might as well have been a sandbank
Of the river that child came from,
Body-exhausted and healing while we held
Our baby in our arms—"Big Fish"
Blinking up at me, her life in my hands,
My Lover holding my hand, this child
A gift of the water we hold hard to everyday
And must learn, one day, to let go.

ADDITIONAL ACKNOWLEDGMENTS

Todich'ii'nii to my wife, Karen, who helped me write this book and nursed me back to health long before we were an item. I can't believe you are my wife. Quyanaq to Eli, Otis, and Sili for allowing me to choose them and for choosing, every day, to be my little ones. Quyanaqpak, Donna, for being our amazing Aaka.

Thank you, Judy Jordan, for your dedicated mentorship and friendship and for providing me a safe space to live, grieve, and write that sparked the idea of living in a tent and made this book possible. Thank you to Allison Joseph, Rodney Jones, and everyone at the MFA Program in Creative Writing at Southern Illinois University Carbondale. Thank you John and Beth Interlandi for your most important friendship. Thank you to DJ and Myla Rosebaugh for supporting me in my various quests, in particular the quest for a full, well-rounded life. Thank you to Jeff Harden for being my poetry papa. Thank you and rest in peace, Dr. Lisa Leslie; your Ecological Literature Class at Virginia Tech changed me forever. Thank you, Henry Ralph Rowe, for taking care of Dr. Leslie in ways no one else could. Thank you to all my clients who trust me to help them tell their stories and allow me to live the life of a poet.

Thank you to all of the friends and strangers who opened their homes to me when I was at my darkest: Kurtis Hessel; Andy, Jessica, Annabel, and Anderson Woodward; Jenny, Paul, and Lily Staab; Annie, Mat, and Bruno Frazier; and John and Kathleern Harkey. If I've missed anyone, feel free to publicly scold me!

Trish and Middle Passage: Everyday I wish you were still with us.

I know I'm not supposed to say that, but it's true. Please pause all that fun you're having in the afterdeath and come visit me again sometime. It's been a while.

Much of this book was written at Don Bubenzer's cabin in the middle-of-nowhere Indiana; you deserve special thanks. The same is true of the Starbucks in Los Osos, CA; thank you for allowing me to sip a single drip coffee all day in the "vault" while writing this book. Thank yous must be expressed to the Owsley Fork Writers' Sanctuary where this book was polished and then finished and polished again and finished again, etc, etc... To Owsley Fork's proprietors, my partners in crime, Linda Bryant, lover of Keanu and verse, and Coleman Davis, waterer of forests, savior of trees: my gratitude. I would be terribly remiss not to thank, from the depths of my heart, the Infinity Fellowship. I can't say enough about rev jeff carr, Kenetha Carr, the Carr kids, and all the amazing people at the only "church" I've ever felt was home. Without the undying support of Denise, Demetrius, DJ, Star, Tanya, Tony, Alicia, Lakesha, Shabaz, Letimicia, Craig, Denzel, Tazia, Nakita, Thea, Tre, Terrence, Carmen, N'Biya, Woo, Joanna, Courtney, Tia, Marissa, Destini, Shae, Nelly, and many others I apologize for failing to list, this book would not exist. I see you...but you don't really hear me tho...

Thank you to Sara Henning and Kimberly Verhines for believing in me and in this book. Thank you to Siolo Thompson for the original painting that graces this book's cover. Thank you to Emily Williams and the rest of the SFA staff for helping bring this book from word doc to bookshelf. Thank you, Lauren Crawford. Thank you, CMarie Fuhrman, Martha Solano, Ken Ilgunas, and Cyrus Cassells.

KAREN CARR

ANDREW MCFADYEN-KETCHUM is an award-winning author, editor, & ghostwriter. He is author of three poetry collections, *Fight or Flight*, *Visiting Hours*, & *Ghost Gear*; Assistant Director of the Owsley Fork Writer's Sanctuary; Founder and Editor of PoemoftheWeek.com; and Acquisitions Editor for Upper Rubber Boot Books. He lives with his wife, Karen, and their three children, Eli, Otis, and Siliuna, in his hometown of Nashville, TN. Learn more at AndrewMK.com.